A TRUE BOOK™

Abraham Lincoln

PETER BENOIT

Children's Press®
An Imprint of Scholastic Inc.
New York   Toronto   London   Auckland   Sydney
Mexico City   New Delhi   Hong Kong
Danbury, Connecticut

Content Consultant
James Marten, PhD
Professor and Chair, History Department
Marquette University
Milwaukee, Wisconsin

Library of Congress Cataloging-in-Publication Data

Benoit, Peter, 1955–
  Abraham Lincoln / Peter Benoit.
      p. cm.—(A true book)
  Includes bibliographical references and index.
  ISBN-13: 978-0-531-26308-2 (lib. bdg.)   ISBN-13: 978-0-531-26621-2 (pbk.)
  ISBN-10: 0-531-26308-8 (lib. bdg.)   ISBN-10: 0-531-26621-4 (pbk.)
  1. Lincoln, Abraham, 1809–1865—Juvenile literature. 2. Presidents—United States—Biography—
Juvenile literature. I. Title. II. Series.
  E457.905.B465 2011
  973.7092—dc22 [B]   2011008350

All rights reserved. Published in 2012 by Children's Press, an imprint of Scholastic Inc.
Printed in China 62
SCHOLASTIC, CHILDREN'S PRESS, A TRUE BOOK, and associated logos are trademarks and/or registered trademarks of Scholastic Inc.
1 2 3 4 5 6 7 8 9 10 R 21 20 19 18 17 16 15 14 13 12

Find the Truth!

Everything you are about to read is true *except* for one of the sentences on this page.

Which one is **TRUE**?

T or F   Lincoln won a seat on the Illinois state legislature the first time he ran for office.

T or F   Lincoln is the only U.S. president to hold a patent.

LINCOLN ★ DOUGLAS DEBATE

AUGUST · 27TH · WEST CHICAGO

Find the answers in this book.

Contents

THE BIG TRUTH!

Lincoln in American Life

Lincoln on the $5 bill

The Union army had more
than 9,100 soldiers who
were under 18 years old.

5

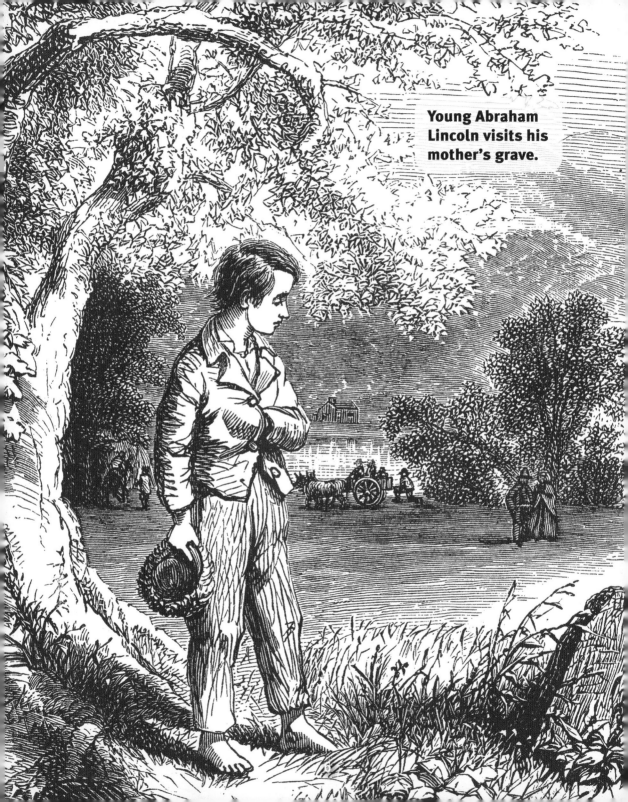

Young Abraham Lincoln visits his mother's grave.

CHAPTER 1

The Making of "Honest Abe"

Abraham Lincoln was named after his grandfather, a **frontier** settler killed by a Native American while working on his Kentucky farm. His grandfather's son Mordecai killed the Indian and saved the family's children. Among them was Tom, Mordecai's younger brother. Tom grew up to be a religious man and respected farmer. On February 12, 1809, his wife, Nancy, gave birth to Abraham in their one-room cabin.

Lincoln's mother died at only 34 years of age.

Childhood

Young Abraham Lincoln led a painful life. At age nine, he nearly drowned, and his mother died from drinking spoiled milk. Ten years later, his older sister, Sarah, died giving birth.

Lincoln's father remarried, and his new wife encouraged Abraham to read. Abe had only 18 months of schooling, but read as many books as he could. He devoted most of the rest of his time to frontier chores such as splitting rails and building fences.

From a young age, Abraham Lincoln enjoyed reading.

Lincoln walked back to Illinois after his trip to New Orleans.

Lincoln's boat trip to New Orleans gave him a chance to experience new parts of the country.

On His Own

In 1830, Tom Lincoln moved his family to Macon County, Illinois. After their arrival, Abraham survived a case of malaria, a serious illness that causes fever and chills. The next year, Tom moved again. Abraham, now 22 years old, decided to go out on his own. He and two friends piloted a boatload of goods from New Salem, Illinois, down the Mississippi River to New Orleans for store owner Denton Offutt. There, Lincoln witnessed southern slavery for the first time.

When Lincoln returned to New Salem, he ran Offutt's general store. A story was told that Lincoln accidentally charged a customer too much and traveled many miles to repay the man. People began calling Lincoln "Honest Abe." The story is probably a myth, but Lincoln, a hard worker and a good storyteller, became well liked. Standing six feet four inches (193 centimeters) tall, he could also be a tough opponent in local wrestling contests.

Lincoln's height made him a strong wrestler.

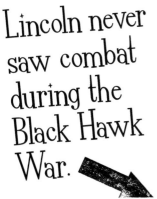
Lincoln never saw combat during the Black Hawk War.

Lincoln joined the militia during the Black Hawk War.

Losing One, Winning One

In 1832, Lincoln became a captain in the Illinois **militia**. Later that year, he lost an election for the Illinois state **legislature**. Even though he lost, people in the area got to know and like him during the **campaign**. He soon got jobs as postmaster and county surveyor. In 1834, he ran again and won. On his first day at work, he arrived in a suit he had bought with borrowed money.

11

Lincoln served four terms in the state legislature. During that time, he studied law, and in 1837, he became a lawyer. A year earlier, he had met Stephen Douglas, another young politician. Years later, Lincoln and Douglas became famed political opponents. Their clashes on the subject of

Stephen Douglas became one of Lincoln's main political rivals.

slavery would help shape the nation's thinking on that bitterly divisive topic. Lincoln opposed slavery, but he thought **abolition** was impractical.

Personal Life

In 1842, Lincoln married Mary Todd, the daughter of a Kentucky banker and slaveholder. Though his wife's ties to slavery bothered Lincoln, he liked her family. Abraham and Mary had four children, Robert, Edward, William, and Tad. Only Robert lived past his teens. The loss of his sons worsened the depression, or deep sadness, that Lincoln battled until the end of his life.

Lincoln once broke off his engagement to Mary Todd.

Like Lincoln, Mary Todd was born in Kentucky and later moved to Illinois.

As a lawyer, Lincoln argued many kinds of cases, including murder trials.

CHAPTER 2

A Purpose Discovered

Lincoln served in the U.S. House of Representatives from 1846 to 1848. Then he continued his law career in Springfield, Illinois, traveling throughout the state handling many kinds of cases. Because of his background piloting riverboats, some of his cases involved transportation issues. In 1849, Lincoln received a **patent** for a device that lifted stranded boats off sandbars. He is the only U.S. president to hold a patent.

Lincoln partnered with a number of other lawyers while working as an attorney.

A pro-slavery group made a raid on Lawrence, Kansas, on May 21, 1856, destroying an antislavery newspaper and hotel.

The Kansas-Nebraska Act brought about major conflict between antislavery and pro-slavery groups.

Lincoln returned to politics when the Kansas-Nebraska Act of 1854 threatened to spread slavery to new territories. Stephen Douglas, now an Illinois senator, claimed that only the residents of a new territory should decide whether to allow slavery in that territory. He believed the U.S. government had no say in the matter. Lincoln disagreed. Although he did not at the time favor abolition, Lincoln opposed creating new slave states. The Republican Party supported his position.

A House Divided

In 1858, Illinois Republicans chose Lincoln as their candidate for senator. During his campaign, he stated that the United States could not remain half-slave and half-free. It must be one or the other. From August through October, he debated Douglas, the Democratic Party candidate, throughout Illinois. The debates attracted national attention. Lincoln lost the election, but it was not the last time he would run for political office.

The Lincoln-Douglas debates helped to make Lincoln known across the country.

Lincoln received strong support from northern voters.

The Election of 1860

Republicans chose Lincoln to run for president in 1860. Douglas again ran against Lincoln with support from northern Democrats. Southern Democrats supported John Breckinridge. On November 6, Lincoln won the election, capturing every northern and midwestern state except New Jersey, which was split between him and Douglas. Believing Lincoln meant to destroy slavery, slave states began to **secede** from the Union.

Slavery

In the 1850s, slavery was the most important
issue in America. The South's **economy** depended
on the forced, unpaid labor of enslaved Africans
to grow cotton, rice, and other crops. By 1860,
about 3.95 million slaves lived in the United
States. Southerners attempted to expand slavery
to territories seeking statehood. Congress passed
laws that made northerners return slaves who had
escaped. Slave and
non-slave states
were on opposite
ends of a bitter
struggle.

Fort Sumter was one of the few remaining U.S. military posts on Confederate soil.

CHAPTER 3

Saving the Union

South Carolina seceded from the Union in December 1860. By February 1861, six more states seceded. They formed a new government, the Confederate States of America. Within a few months, four more states joined the Confederacy. Lincoln was sworn in as president on March 4, 1861. Four weeks later, Confederate troops fired on U.S. soldiers at Fort Sumter, South Carolina. The U.S. troops were forced to surrender. The American Civil War had begun.

Not a single soldier died on either side during the attack on Fort Sumter.

Militia groups did their best to protect Union cities from rioting during the beginning of the war.

In calling for a naval blockade and requesting aid from militias, Lincoln exercised rights that no other president had before.

Lincoln immediately summoned U.S., or Union, troops to defend Washington, D.C. On April 19, Lincoln ordered the U.S. Navy to block access to 12 Southern ports. His decisive actions eventually kept foreign nations from shipping weapons to the South. It also prevented the Confederacy from receiving other goods and from selling cotton in Europe. This limited the amount of supplies and funds the Confederates had to fight the war.

The House Divides

Both the United States and the
Confederacy believed they could
quickly win the conflict. Instead,
the war would last four years.
Families were split apart.
Brothers, cousins, and friends
fought against each other in
bloody battles. Early in the war,
Lincoln was unable to find a
general who could lead the Union
to a speedy victory. In the East,
Confederate troops pounded their
Union foes, even threatening
Washington, D.C.

**By law, soldiers had to be 18, but
many boys on both sides lied about
their age. Soldiers as young as 13
fought and died in the war.**

Carrying a Heavy Weight

Lincoln was constantly attacked by Northern politicians. Northern Democrats wanted him to make peace. Radical Republicans insisted that the president abolish slavery. Lincoln believed that the war was needed to preserve the Union, not destroy slavery. He also feared that freeing the slaves would push the states bordering the South to join the Confederacy.

This map shows the Union and Confederate states during the Civil War (1861–1865).

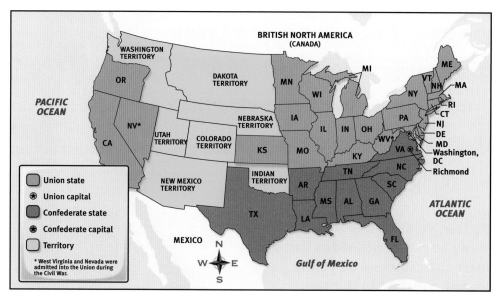

Battlefield defeats and constant political fighting added to Lincoln's woes. Then, in early 1862, he suffered a personal loss when his 11-year-old son, Willie, died. Lincoln sank into another deep depression. As time passed, he began to embrace the idea of **emancipation**, or freeing the slaves. But he could not make such a bold move while the Union seemed to be losing the war. Many Northerners would not support him.

Three of Lincoln's four sons died before reaching adulthood.

This photograph of Willie Lincoln was taken in 1861.

The Emancipation Proclamation was an important step toward permanently ending slavery.

The Emancipation Proclamation

On September 17, 1862, Union forces defeated Confederate soldiers at the Battle of Antietam in Maryland. The victory gave Lincoln the confidence to issue the Emancipation Proclamation. It stated that as of January 1, 1863, all slaves living in rebel, or Confederate, states were free. Slaves in Union-controlled areas were not covered by the proclamation. Though not technically free, they were often not living as slaves at the time.

The Emancipation Proclamation also did not free slaves in the border states, which were pro-Union. Doing so might have driven those states into the Confederacy, which would have been a huge loss of territory and resources for the Union. Emancipation, however, did change Americans' attitudes toward the war. Now, preserving the Union went hand in hand with the goal of permanently ending slavery.

Slaves on plantations taken over by Union soldiers were often allowed to live as free people.

The Emancipation Proclamation allowed the Union to recruit about 180,000 black soldiers during the war. ➡

Lincoln in American Life

In the years since his death, Abraham Lincoln has become a larger-than-life figure. Many modern historians consider him the greatest U.S. president. Lincoln's words and actions have had a long lasting impact on how Americans think of themselves and their country. Americans continue to honor him today in many ways.

Five-Dollar Bill

Lincoln's image began appearing on $5 bills in 1914. In 2008, the new version of the $5 bill featured an image of Lincoln taken in 1864 by famed Civil War photographer Mathew Brady.

Lincoln Penny

In 1909, the 100th anniversary of Lincoln's birth, the U.S. government replaced its Indian Head Penny with a profile of the late president. The Lincoln Memorial was shown on the back of the penny from 1959 to 2008.

Lincoln Memorial

Work on a national monument to honor Lincoln began in 1914. Designed by Henry Bacon, the Lincoln Memorial in Washington, D.C., features a sculpture of the president that is 19 feet (5.8 meters) tall. President Warren G. Harding and Lincoln's son, Robert, attended the memorial's dedication ceremony in 1922.

After the battle at Gettysburg, wagons were wheeled through the battle site to carry away wounded soldiers.

CHAPTER 4

A Hard Road to Victory

In summer 1863, Confederate commander Robert E. Lee invaded the North. Lee had won many battles against the Union and seemed impossible to defeat. Union leader George Meade was new to his command. The armies clashed at Gettysburg, Pennsylvania, from July 1 to 3. Each side had more than 23,000 men killed and wounded. The Union won the struggle, which was the bloodiest battle of the war.

Meade angered Lincoln when he failed to chase Lee's forces after the battle.

More people died in the Civil War than in any other war in American history.

Gettysburg marked a turning point in the war. The Union had pushed back what would be the Confederates' final invasion of the North. The Union still had the manpower and resources to continue fighting, but each battle drained the Confederacy. Lincoln's plan was now to wear down the Confederates in battle after battle. Ulysses S. Grant, the commanding general of the Union army, carried this plan through.

The Gettysburg Address

In early November 1863, Lincoln was invited to speak at a national cemetery in memory of those killed at Gettysburg. On November 19, he began his now-famous speech with the phrase "Four score and seven years ago." This referred back to the Declaration of Independence, signed in 1776, 87 (four score and seven) years before. Lincoln delivered his short speech in about three minutes. In it, Lincoln powerfully conveyed that the terrible war was the price America had to pay for freedom and equality.

Lincoln was unhappy with his speech at Gettysburg and called it a "flat failure."

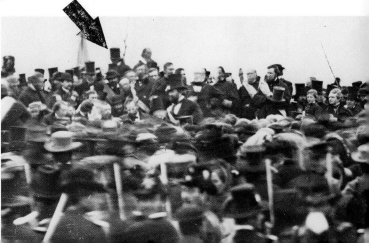

The Gettysburg Address was delivered to about 15,000 people.

The Reelection Campaign

By mid-1864, the war raged on. Tens of thousands more soldiers died. There did not seem to be an end in sight to the killing. Lincoln's popularity dropped. His fellow Republicans doubted if he could win reelection in the fall. Even Lincoln admitted he might lose. Democrats were split between those who wanted to continue the war and those who demanded an immediate peace with the Southern states.

Timeline of Abraham Lincoln's Life

1809
Lincoln is born in Kentucky.

1858
Lincoln and Stephen Douglas debate.

In summer 1864, news from the battlefield boosted Lincoln's chances. Grant had pinned enemy forces against the Confederate capital of Richmond, Virginia. Lee was unable to defend the city, and more Union troops were arriving. Later that year, Union general William Tecumseh Sherman led his forces from Atlanta, Georgia, to Savannah, on Georgia's coast. As they marched, they destroyed everything in their path. Lincoln's popularity surged. In the 1864 presidential election, he won all but three states.

1861
The American Civil War begins at Fort Sumter.

1865
Lincoln is shot and killed while attending a play.

Many former slaves served in the Union army during the Civil War.

CHAPTER 5

Victory and Tragedy

The Emancipation Proclamation had allowed the Union army to accept former slaves as soldiers. But Lincoln had used special presidential powers granted only during wartime to end slavery. He would lose this power when the war ended. He feared the Emancipation Proclamation might be overturned. Lincoln began to gather support for an **amendment** to the U.S. Constitution that would permanently put an end to slavery.

By the end of the war, the Union army was about 10 percent black.

General Lee surrendered to General Grant at Appomattox Court House.

General Lee sits between his son (left) and his military aide (right), after returning home from Appomattox.

End of the War

Despite heavy Union losses, Grant had battered Lee's forces in Virginia. On April 9, 1865, Lee tried to fight his way past Grant at Appomattox, Virginia. His attempt failed, and Lee surrendered his army later the same day. The rest of the Confederate army soon surrendered as well. The American Civil War was over.

Other Business

Although Abraham Lincoln is best remembered for preserving the Union, he signed a number of important laws unrelated to the war or slavery. The Homestead Act of 1862 gave settlers up to 160 acres (65 hectares) of free land west of the Mississippi River. In 1862 and 1864, he supported the building of the first railway across the United States. Lincoln also declared a Thanksgiving Day in November, which became the holiday we celebrate today.

The Homestead Act encouraged movement west for years after it was passed.

Constitutional Amendment

The antislavery amendment that Lincoln desired passed the House of Representatives in January 1865. For the amendment to become law, it needed approval in the Senate by 27 states (there were 36 at that time). On February 1, Illinois became the first state to vote for approval. On April 14, Arkansas became the 21st to vote for its passage. That evening, Lincoln and his wife, Mary, attended a play at Ford's Theatre in Washington, D.C.

There was great excitement in the House of Representatives when the 13th Amendment was passed.

John Wilkes Booth had several accomplices in his assassination of the president.

A Fatal Shot

During a pause in the play, Lincoln's bodyguard stepped away from his post at the president's box seats. A pro-Confederate actor named John Wilkes Booth, determined to **assassinate** the president, entered the box. He shot Lincoln in the head, leapt to the stage, and ran out a side door. Lincoln was immediately carried to a house across the street. He died the next morning at 7:22 a.m. Twelve days later, soldiers trapped and killed Booth on a Virginia farm.

Lincoln's funeral train traveled 1,654 miles (2,662 km) from Washington, D.C., to Springfield, Illinois.

After his death, Lincoln's body was put aboard a train that would take him to his burial place in Springfield, Illinois. Along the way, an estimated 1.3 million mourners viewed his body. In May, Lincoln was buried in Springfield's Oak Ridge Cemetery. In December, Georgia became the 27th state to approve the 13th Amendment, the law that abolished slavery. Lincoln had died saving his nation and having changed it forever. ★

Number of months of schooling Lincoln had as a child: 18

Number of Lincoln-Douglas debates: 7

Number of slaves in the United States in 1860: About 3.95 million

Number of dead and wounded at the Battle of Gettysburg: At least 46,000

Number of words in the Gettysburg Address: Fewer than 300

Number of soldiers who died in the Civil War: More than 360,000

Estimated number of people who saw Lincoln's funeral train pass by: 12 milion

Did you find the truth?

F Lincoln won a seat in the Illinois state legislature the first time he ran for office.

T Lincoln is the only U.S. president to hold a patent.

Resources

Books

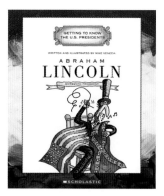

Fontes, Justine, and Ron Fontes. *Abraham Lincoln: Lawyer, Leader, Legend*. New York: DK Children, 2009.

Fradin, Dennis B. *The Assassination of Abraham Lincoln*. New York: Benchmark, 2007.

Hossell, Karen P. *The Gettysburg Address*. Chicago: Heinemann-Raintree, 2006.

Mattern, Joanne. *Mary Todd Lincoln*. Edina, MN: Checkerboard, 2008.

Rappaport, Doreen. *Abe's Honest Words: The Life of Abraham Lincoln*. New York: Hyperion, 2008.

Rivera, Sheila. *The Gettysburg Address*. Edina, MN: ABDO and Daughters, 2004.

Stone, Tanya Lee. *Abraham Lincoln*. New York: DK Children, 2005.

Venezia, Mike. *Abraham Lincoln: Sixteenth President*. New York: Children's Press, 2005.

Organizations and Web Sites

Library of Congress: Abraham Lincoln Papers

http://memory.loc.gov/ammem/alhtml/malhome.html
View a copy of the Emancipation Proclamation and the
Gettysburg Address plus many other important papers written
by Lincoln from the 1850s until his death in 1865.

The Lincoln Archives Digital Project

www.lincolnarchives.us
Study maps, papers, photographs, and other historical records
found at the National Archives and put on this private Web site.

Places to Visit

Abraham Lincoln Presidential Museum

212 N. Sixth Street
Springfield, IL 62701
(217) 558-8934
www.alplm.org/home.html
Learn about Lincoln's life
and work, see photos and
films, and explore a hands-on
children's area.

Ford's Theatre National Historic Site

511 Tenth Street, NW
Washington, DC 20004
(202) 347-4833
www.fordstheatre.org
Visit the theater where John
Wilkes Booth shot Lincoln,
and find out more about
the 16th president and the
Civil War.

Important Words

abolition (ab-uh-LIH-shuhn) — the official end of something

amendment (uh-MEND-muhnt) — a change that is made to a law or legal document

assassinate (us-SAS-uh-nayt) — to murder a well-known person

campaign (kam-PAYN) — a planned series of actions designed to win an election

economy (ih-KA-ne-mee) — the system of buying, selling, and making things and managing money

emancipation (i-man-suh-PAY-shun) — freeing a person or group from slavery

frontier (fruhn-TEER) — the far edge of a settled territory or country

legislature (LEJ-is-lay-chur) — a body with the power to make or change the laws

militia (muh-LISH-uh) — a group of people who are trained to fight but who aren't professional soldiers

patent (PAT-uhnt) — a document that gives an inventor the exclusive right to make or sell an invention

secede (si-SEED) — to withdraw formally from a group or organization

Index

Page numbers in **bold** indicate illustrations

About the Author

Peter Benoit is educated as a mathematician but has many other interests. He has taught and tutored high school and college students for many years, mostly in math and science. He also runs summer workshops for writers and students of literature. Mr. Benoit has also written more than 2,000 poems. His life has been one committed to learning. He lives in Greenwich, New York.